WHO KNEW?

THE WONDERS OF
BIOMIMICRY

KATHLEEN E. MADDEN

TILBURY HOUSE PUBLISHERS

TILBURY HOUSE PUBLISHERS™

an imprint of
Cherry Lake Publishing Group
2395 South Huron Parkway, Suite 200
Ann Arbor, MI 48104

www.tilburyhouse.com

Library of Congress Cataloging-in-Publication Data

Names: Madden, Kathleen E., author.
Title: Who knew : the wonders of biomimicry / Kathleen E. Madden.
Description: Ann Arbor : Tilbury House Publishers, 2024. | Audience: Ages 4–9 | Summary: "Sometimes nature is the world's greatest innovator. From butterfly wings to kingfisher birds, nature has been inspiring humans to build better and smarter for generations. This introduction to biomimicry is filled with stunning photographs and amazing facts to encourage engagement and spark curiosity in early readers"– Provided by publisher.
Identifiers: LCCN 2024011327 | ISBN 9780884489931 (hardcover)
Subjects: LCSH: Mimicry (Biology)–Juvenile literature.
Classification: LCC QH546 .M24 2024 | DDC 578.4/7–dc23/eng/20240524
LC record available at https://lccn.loc.gov/2024011327

10 9 8 7 6 5 4 3 2 1

Working with Nature

Making New Discoveries

For the past 3.77 billion years, the natural world has been constantly working to adapt and improve in order to survive. From the first spark of life to the present, it has been a forward journey toward invention and perfection. The changes that occur in plant, animal, and human species over time is called *evolution*.

Animals and plants were on earth about 495 million years before humans arrived. They faced many challenges and went through many changes to survive. Today, we are taking a leaf from nature's book to solve human problems. This is called *biomimicry*. Biologists work with product designers, engineers, and architects to make new products or improve on older ones.

Although many plants and animals have died out or become extinct because of disease, many have disappeared due to humans. Now, when we look to nature to solve our problems, we realize how important it is to preserve it. We wouldn't want to lose something that may be able to help us in the future.

This book is about biomimicry.
"What is biomimicry?" you may ask.

bi•o•mim•ic•ry (BY-oh-MIM-ehk-ree)

noun: the design and creation of materials, buildings, and processes that are modeled on nature

---

Examples:

 The reflective quality of a cat's eyes led to reflective traffic signs.

 Moths' eyes inspired a surface that could be used on smartphones or tablets to cut down on glare from the sun or bright lights.

 Current research into the way hummingbirds fly might help developers design wings for tiny drones.

Ants showed an airline how to move cargo and board passengers faster—and save money.

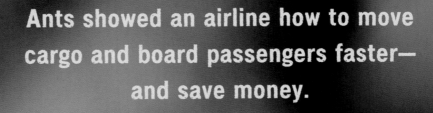

People today always seek a better, more efficient, and less expensive way of doing business. When trying to solve the problems facing an airline, computer engineers studied an ant colony. Ants have rules they follow to survive. Computer programmers designed algorithms—rules a computer can follow to help solve complicated problems quickly—that work like ant rules. These algorithms helped an airline move cargo more efficiently—and at a lower cost—to board passengers faster.

Ants learned to survive and thrive by working together for hundreds of millions of years. They developed something called *swarm intelligence.* Each ant has a specific job, and they all work together to survive.

Bats inspired improvements to the ways robots move.

Bats fly at night and eat large quantities of insects—as many as 6,000 to 8,000 bugs per bat each night.

Instead of eyesight, bats use echolocation to find prey. They send out sound waves that can't be heard by humans, called ultrasound. Scientists used high-speed video to find out how the bats used ultrasound and echolocation to hunt. They discovered that when the bat's sound wave hits something, like an insect, it bounces back to the bat, telling the bat right where the insect is. Now scientists are using this discovery to improve robots. For example, robotic lawn mowers use ultrasonic sensors to detect and avoid obstacles—just like bats.

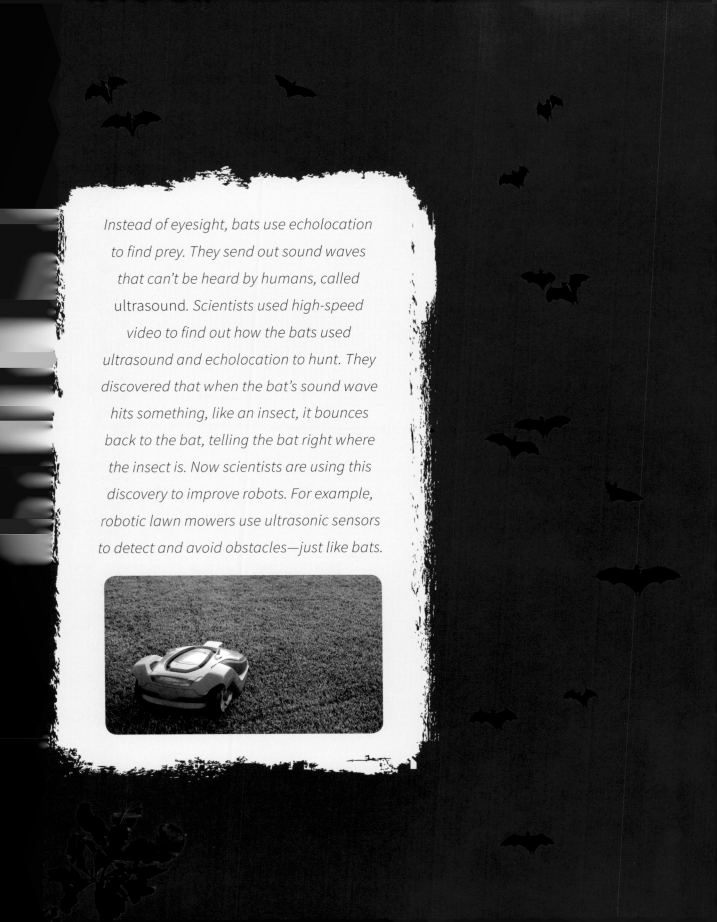

Burdock seeds led to the invention of Velcro®.

Burdock is a plant that grows wild in many places around the world. The root is used as medicine in some places and eaten as food in Asia. Most animals don't eat it because the plant is covered in prickly burrs.

After looking at burdock seeds under a microscope, one inventor noticed that there were little hooks on the tips of the seeds. Could this be why the prickly burrs clung to his dog's fur? After ten years of trial and error, he came up with Velcro®.

Butterfly wings led to better cell phone screens.

The wings of the blue morpho butterfly are covered by a complex pattern of thousands of tiny scales. The arrangement of the pattern reflects light and gives the butterflies their vivid, iridescent color.

Computer hardware engineers copied the unique pattern and design of these butterfly wings to build new display screens. This allowed them to make brighter, more readable screens on smartphones, tablets, and gaming devices.

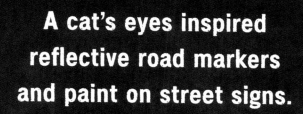

A cat's eyes inspired reflective road markers and paint on street signs.

Animals that go out at night, such as cats, have a unique reflective surface in the backs of their eyes which makes their eyes seem to glow. This allows them to see better in the dark. In 1934, an inventor out for a drive noticed the way a cat's eyes were gleaming in the dark as it stood alongside the road. This quick observation inspired him to create the first reflective road markers.

Embedding markers in the center of the road helps drivers stay within their lanes. Reflective street signs make it easier to find our way. Both have improved the safety of driving.

Coral reefs are helping engineers design better building materials.

Coral reefs are underwater homes to many marine animals. Reefs are made of thin layers of calcium carbonate. Tiny animals called *coral polyps* take carbon from seawater and decaying algae and turn it into the chalky substance (calcium carbonate) that forms the reefs over time.

Engineers used reef biomimicry to make a new type of cement. They studied how polyps make reefs, and found a way to combine the carbon dioxide emissions from a power plant with seawater. This created their own calcium carbonate cement. The cement led to stronger, lighter building materials.

Dragonflies' supersight is inspiring new ways for robots to see.

Dragonflies have enormous compound eyes. Each eye contains 30,000 facets. They also have three small eyes, called *ocelli*, that send information to the dragonfly's motor center. This allows them to react very quickly. Dragonflies have nearly 360-degree vision, with just one blind spot behind them.

Robotic engineers are working on a similar design of faceted eyes working with more simple ocelli. This system will help robots detect and track small objects against a busy background, like how a dragonfly sees.

Giraffes helped solve one of the problems of human space travel.

A giraffe's legs are six feet long. This would be a problem for the human cardiovascular system, but gravity doesn't cause blood to collect and make a giraffe's legs swell. Unlike humans, giraffes have very tight skin on their legs that squeezes them and helps regulate blood pressure—like the LBNP device!

When astronauts travel in space, they become weightless. This changes how their bodies work. Without gravity, all the blood is squeezed into their heads. Upon reentry, their legs and ankles fill with blood. This often meant astronauts would black out as they traveled back to Earth. The invention of the lower body negative pressure (LBNP) *device solved this problem. It works like a vacuum cleaner by applying negative pressure over the lower body while in space—keeping the blood from rushing to the head—and stops homecoming astronauts from blacking out. The LBNP device was developed after studying giraffes.*

Hummingbirds can hover in place and fly backward— inspiring drone flight.

Most birds flap their wings up and down to create lift on the downstroke. Hummingbirds move their wings in figure eights to maintain constant lift. This allows them to make very controlled movements.

Researchers are hoping the study of hummingbird flight will help engineers design flying drones that are lighter, more efficient, and easier to maneuver.

The beak of the kingfisher bird led to the sleek shape of the bullet train.

The kingfisher bird has a large head, a long, sharply pointed bill, short legs, and a tail. The shape of their sleek bill lets them catch fish under water without making a splash (which would scare the fish away).

Engineers at the Japanese Rail network mimicked the shape of the kingfisher's beak to redesign the bullet train. The new design let the train disturb less air as it moved. This solved noise problems, increased energy efficiency, and allowed the trains to go even faster.

Lobster vision inspired a low-powered X-ray device that can see through steel.

Lobsters have an almost unlimited field of vision. Their eyes pop out from their heads to see images on all sides at the same time. Each cell in the eye captures a small amount of light from different angles. Then the light is combined to form a single image. This helps lobsters to see in dark and murky water.

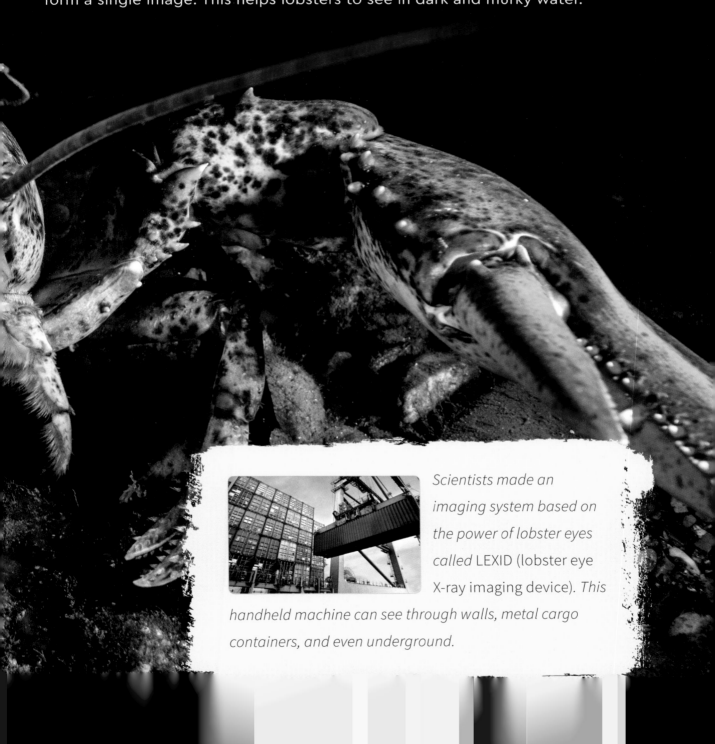

Scientists made an imaging system based on the power of lobster eyes called LEXID (lobster eye X-ray imaging device). *This handheld machine can see through walls, metal cargo containers, and even underground.*

Lotus leaves are inspiring fabrics that shed dirt and water.

Waxy crystalloids on lotus plants make the leaves water repellent. The crystalloids also have a rough surface—though it's so small, you wouldn't notice it without a microscope. So as water beads off the leaves, the rough surface dislodges dirt and washes it off the leaves as well. This makes the lotus plant self-cleaning.

New fabrics are being developed with similar self-cleaning abilities thanks to the observation of these plants by biologists and engineers.

The surface of the moth's eye inspired a coating that could be used on mobile displays to reduce glare from sunlight.

Moths have a special dull coating on their eyes, making it harder for the moth to be seen at night by predators.

Researchers have developed a textured film inspired by those dull, nonreflective moth eyes. When the film is applied to mobile screens, it would not only make the screen easier to see but reduce the drain on the battery.

Pitcher plants inspired a new nonstick surface.

Pitcher plants are carnivorous. They capture insects and tiny frogs that fall into their tube-shaped leaves. The creatures can't climb out because the inside of the plant is slippery. The prey decomposes inside and feeds the plant.

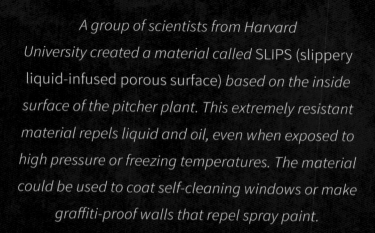

A group of scientists from Harvard University created a material called SLIPS (slippery liquid-infused porous surface) *based on the inside surface of the pitcher plant. This extremely resistant material repels liquid and oil, even when exposed to high pressure or freezing temperatures. The material could be used to coat self-cleaning windows or make graffiti-proof walls that repel spray paint.*

Polar bear fur is hollow and waterproof— inspiring a super material for space travel.

Polar bears live in the Arctic, one of the most extreme parts of the planet. They have adapted in several ways to survive the very cold weather. They have black skin under their fur, which helps them absorb sunlight efficiently. They have a thick layer of fat to stay warm, even in the icy water. They also have a unique type of fur with long and hollow hairs. It helps them stay afloat when swimming and holds in the heat to provide insulation.

Inspired by polar bears, researchers have made a material of tiny hollow nanotubes. The material is lightweight, water resistant, and a super insulator. Researchers are working to perfect this new material for use in the aerospace industry.

Porcupine quills inspired medical staples.

Porcupines are large rodents covered with about 30,000 quills. The quills are very sharp and protect the porcupines from predators.

Bioengineers are studying porcupine quills in the hope of creating better surgical staples. Current staples cause damage to patients' tissue. The opening of the wound can lead to infections. Porcupine quills have fine backward-facing hooks, or barbs, on their tips. Those barbs make it easier for the quills to slide into predators' skin but hard to come out. Quills are sharper than a hypodermic needle and could help the patient heal faster. The engineered staples would dissolve over time, eliminating the need for a follow-up appointment to remove them.

Seashells inspired a new shatter-resistant design for glass.

Several mollusk species have shells lined with an inner iridescent layer called *nacre*, also known as mother-of-pearl. This material is especially tough.

Scientists studied how nacre could be both rigid and durable simultaneously. They found that it is made up of many layers of stiff calcium carbonate and elastic soft proteins. They duplicated this structure in the lab with layers of glass flakes and acrylic. The new material is five times more shatter resistant than regular glass.

Termites inspired better building designs for a warming planet.

Termites build mud homes called *mounds*. These mounds can reach almost thirty feet tall. The mounds maintain steady temperatures due to intricate systems of tunnels and chimneys that the termites can open and close throughout the day to create drafts. The cool air at the mound's base moves up and out of the top.

The Eastgate Centre, Zimbabwe's most well-known office and shopping complex, used design methods based on termite mounds. The architect and engineers created a building that maintains a comfortable temperature without using typical air-conditioning and heating systems. Instead, the air is drawn into the first floor with fans, is vented throughout the building, and then exits through chimneys at the top. The Eastgate Centre uses around 90 percent less energy than most buildings its size.

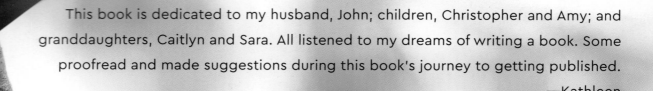

This book is dedicated to my husband, John; children, Christopher and Amy; and granddaughters, Caitlyn and Sara. All listened to my dreams of writing a book. Some proofread and made suggestions during this book's journey to getting published.

—Kathleen

Kathleen Madden is an author, artist, community volunteer, and retired graphic designer. Being dyslexic, she is inspired to create books that combine simple text with stunning photography, sparking interest in struggling readers and improving comprehension. Kathleen believes that understanding biomimicry is essential for modern innovation and the preservation of nature.

Photo Credits: © Ondrej Prosicky/Shutterstock, cover, 1; © LedyX/Shutterstock, 2–3; © Ana Prego/Shutterstock, 4–5; © fabien bazanegue/ Unsplash, 5; © Oasishifi/Shutterstock, 6–7; © Jaromir Chalabala/Shutterstock, 6; © serrah galos/Unsplash, 8–9; © Natalya/Envato, 9; © wirestock/Envato, 10–11; © Dobo Kristian/Shutterstock, 11; © Kriachko OleksII/Shutterstock, 12–13; © william hook/Unspash, 12; © Nils Jacobi/Shutterstock, 5, 14–15; © kim7/Shutterstock, 15; © Ethan Daniels/Shutterstock, 16–17; © Songquan Deng/Shutterstock.com, 17; © hoch3media/Unsplash, 18–19; © iLexx/Envato, 19; © nwdph/Shutterstock, 20–21; © Oleg_Yakovlev/Shutterstock, 20; © anchor lee/Unsplash, 5, 22–23; © ricardo gomez angel/Unsplash, 5, 23; © Yakov Oskanov/Envato, 24–25; © SteveAllenPhoto999/Envato, 24; © RLS Photo/ Shutterstock, 26–27; © MOLPIX/Shutterstock, 27; © Praew stock/Shutterstock, 28–29; © vchal/Shutterstock, 28; © R K Hill/Shutterstock, 5, 30–31; © henry ascrof/Unsplash, 5, 31; © leungchopan/Envato, 32–33; © fanjianhua/Shutterstock, 33; © FloridaStock/Shutterstock, 34–35; © Rick Partington/Shutterstock, 35; © skyler ewing/Unsplash, 36–37; © Monkey Business Images/Shutterstock, 37; © dagmara-dombrovska/ Pexels, 38–39; © Steve Mann/Shutterstock, 39; © ingeborg korme/Unsplash, 40–41; © Wikipedia.com, 41; © DennisJacobsen/Envato, 42